Build business not a job: Grow your business and attain financial freedom.

Terry T. McClelland

Introduction

Building a business, not a job, is about creating an entity that operates independently of your constant presence and efforts. While a job ties you to a specific role, often limiting your potential for growth and freedom, a business provides a scalable framework that can grow beyond your individual contributions. By focusing on developing systems, leveraging technology, and cultivating a team that can manage day-to-day operations, you position yourself to enjoy greater flexibility, financial rewards, and long-term sustainability. This approach enables you to innovate, explore new opportunities, and create lasting value, ultimately transforming your entrepreneurial vision into a thriving, autonomous enterprise.

Difference Between a Job and a Business

Understanding the separation between an undertaking and a business is key for business visionaries searching for money-related opportunities and long-short turns of events.

JOB

Dependence on Owner: In an undertaking, the owner's time and capacities are clearly linked to the compensation delivered. When the owner stops working, the compensation stops.

Confined Flexibility: An errand is limited by the number of hours the owner can work. This cap on effort limits improvement potential.

High Affiliation: The owner is locked in with all pieces of everyday exercise, regularly provoking burnout and limited individual adaptability.

Pay Security: Pay is all around stable anyway covered, as it relies only upon the owner's undertakings and hours worked.

BUSINESS

Freedom from Proprietor: A business wants to work and convey pay without the proprietor's dependable thought. Frameworks and social occasions handle ordinary activities.

Adaptability: A business can provoke and oversee broadened interest through scaling endeavours, creating business regions, and utilising improvement.

Task and the Pioneers: The proprietor bases his decisions on major choices, while a social event handles execution. This contemplates the valuable utilisation of assets and limits.

Pay Potential: A business has huge pay potential as it can expand its certificate, increment game plans, and develop different income streams freed from the proprietor's brief endeavours.

By progressing from an endeavour to a business, monetary experts can achieve extra-recognizable independence from a vain day-to-day presence, individual adaptability, and the capacity to scale and encourage their undertaking past private constraints.

Chapter 1: Laying the Foundation

Spreading out significant solid areas is essential while changing from being freely utilised to building a flexible business. This fundamental part dives into the significant perspectives that set the stage for long-term accomplishment.

Describing the vision and mission

The part begins by underscoring the meaning of making a sensible vision and mission statement. Your vision communicates the future you envision for your business, giving a coordinating light that organises your fundamental decisions and moves your gathering. In the meantime, your mission statement describes the inspiration driving your business, outlining how you intend to serve your clients and add to your industry or neighbourhood. Together, these parts spread out a strong design that changes your exercises to your general goals.

Identifying Your Niche

Then, the section investigates the basics of recognizing your specialty market. This includes conducting intensive statistical surveying to comprehend your ideal interest group's necessities, inclinations, and trouble spots. By pinpointing a particular specialty, you can fit your items or administrations to really satisfy concentrated needs. Besides, zeroing in on a specialty permits you to separate your business from rivals, situating yourself as a subject matter expert and possibly directing greater costs for your contributions.

Setting strategic goals

Lastly, laying the foundation entails setting strategic goals for your business. These goals should be SMART (specific, measurable, achievable, relevant, and time-bound) and aligned with your vision and mission. Strategic goals provide a roadmap for growth and enable you to track progress, make informed decisions, and adapt to changing market conditions.

By laying a solid foundation through a clear vision and mission, targeted market identification, and strategic goal-setting, you establish a robust framework that supports the sustainable growth and scalability of your business. This chapter equips you with essential tools and insights to navigate the complexities of entrepreneurship and build a thriving enterprise that transcends individual effort.

Vision and Mission

Vision and mission statements are foundational elements that define the purpose and direction of a business, guiding its growth and strategic decisions.

Vision Statement

A vision statement articulates the long-term aspirations and goals of the business. It serves as a beacon that inspires and motivates stakeholders, including employees, customers, and investors. A compelling vision paints a vivid picture of what the business aims to achieve in the future. It should be ambitious yet realistic, capturing the essence of where the business sees itself in the years to come. A well-crafted vision statement not only outlines tangible objectives, such as market leadership or global expansion, but also reflects the values and principles that drive the organisation forward. It provides clarity and alignment, ensuring that all efforts and initiatives are directed towards a common purpose.

Mission Statement

In contrast, a mission statement focuses on the present-day purpose and core activities of the business. It defines the fundamental reason for the business's existence and outlines how it serves its stakeholders. A mission statement communicates the business's unique value proposition to customers, emphasising the solutions it provides and the benefits it delivers. It also sets expectations for employees by clarifying the company's priorities and guiding principles. A well-defined mission statement is concise, clear, and memorable, encapsulating the essence of the business's operations and its commitment to delivering value.

Together, vision and mission statements provide a framework for strategic planning and decision-making. They unify the organisation around common goals, foster a sense of purpose and direction among employees, and differentiate the business in the marketplace. By articulating a compelling vision and mission, businesses can inspire loyalty, attract top talent, and cultivate a strong corporate identity that resonates with customers and stakeholders alike.

Crafting a Compelling Vision

Crafting a compelling vision for your business is essential for providing direction, inspiration, and alignment throughout your organisation. A vision statement should vividly articulate the future aspirations and goals that you envision for your business. Here's how you can craft a compelling vision:

1. Clarity and Specificity: Clearly define what success looks like for your business in the long term. Whether it's achieving market leadership, transforming an industry, or impacting communities, ensure your vision is specific and understandable to all stakeholders.

2. Inspiration and Motivation: Your vision should inspire and motivate people within and outside the organisation. It should resonate emotionally, stirring passion and commitment among employees, customers, and investors alike.

3. Alignment with Values: Align your vision with the core values and principles that define your business. This ensures authenticity and reinforces the company culture, guiding decision-making and behaviours.

4. Future-Oriented: Look ahead and imagine the possibilities for your business in the next 5, 10, or even 20 years. Anticipate future trends and opportunities, and reflect these aspirations in your vision statement.

5. Realistic Yet Ambitious: Strike a balance between being aspirational and achievable. While your vision should push boundaries and challenge the status quo, it should also be grounded in the current capabilities and resources of your business.

6. Communicate Effectively: Articulate your vision in a concise and memorable manner. Use powerful language that evokes imagery and excitement, making it easy for everyone to understand and rally behind.

By crafting a compelling vision statement, you set a clear path forward for your business, aligning efforts towards a common goal and fostering a sense of purpose among stakeholders. It serves as a guiding star, driving strategic decisions, inspiring innovation, and ultimately propelling your business towards sustainable growth and success in a competitive marketplace.

Chapter 2: Business Planning

Business planning is a foundational process that sets the course for a successful enterprise. It involves systematically outlining goals, strategies, and actions to achieve desired outcomes. Here's an overview of key components in business planning:

1. Setting Goals: Define specific, measurable objectives that align with your business vision. These goals should be realistic yet ambitious, providing a clear direction for growth and success.

2. Market Analysis: Conduct thorough research to understand your target market, industry trends, and competitors. Identify market gaps, customer needs, and opportunities that your business can capitalise on.

3. Strategic Planning: Develop strategies to achieve your goals based on market insights. This includes product development, pricing strategies, distribution channels, and marketing approaches tailored to your target audience.

4. Financial Planning: Outline financial projections, including revenue forecasts, expenses, and cash flow management. Determine startup costs, funding requirements, and profitability targets to ensure financial sustainability.

5. Operational Planning: Define operational processes, organisational structure, and resource allocation. Establish workflows, roles, responsibilities, and systems to streamline operations and enhance efficiency.

6. Risk Management: Identify potential risks and develop contingency plans to mitigate them. This includes market risks, financial risks, regulatory risks, and operational challenges that may impact business continuity.

7. Monitoring and Evaluation: Implement metrics and key performance indicators (KPIs) to track progress towards goals. Regularly review and adjust business strategies based on performance data and market dynamics.

Effective business planning provides a roadmap for navigating challenges, seizing opportunities, and achieving sustainable growth. It aligns stakeholders, guides decision-making, and enhances the overall success and resilience of your business in a competitive environment.

Essential Components of a Business Plan

The essential components of a business plan include key sections that collectively provide a comprehensive roadmap for your business. Here are the crucial elements:

1. Executive Summary: A concise overview of your business concept, goals, and how you plan to achieve them. It highlights the uniqueness of your business and captures the reader's attention.

2. Business Description: Detailed information about your business idea, including its mission, vision, values, legal structure, and location. Describe your products or services and the problems they solve in the market.

3. Market analysis: a thorough examination of your target market, including its size, demographics, needs, trends, and growth potential. Analyse your competitors and identify your unique selling propositions (USPs).

4. Organization and Management: Outline your company's organisational structure, management team, and key personnel. Include the resumes and roles of founders and key employees, highlighting their relevant experience and skills.

5. Product or Service Line: Provide detailed descriptions of your offerings, their features, benefits, and differentiation from competitors. Discuss your development stage, intellectual property, and future product or service plans.

6. Marketing and Sales Strategy: Detail your approach to attracting and retaining customers. Include your target market segments, pricing strategy, distribution channels, promotional tactics, and sales forecast.

7. Funding Request: If seeking funding, specify the amount required, how funds will be used, and potential sources of

financing. Provide financial projections, including income statements, cash flow statements, and balance sheets.

8. Financial Projections: Present realistic financial forecasts for the next 3–5 years. Include revenue projections, expenses, profitability analysis, break-even analysis, and assumptions used to develop these forecasts.

9. Appendix: Include supplementary materials such as resumes, permits, contracts, market research data, and any other relevant documents that support your business plan.

Each component serves a specific purpose in demonstrating the viability and potential of your business idea to stakeholders, whether investors, lenders, or internal teams. Crafting a comprehensive business plan not only helps you clarify your business concept but also prepares you to effectively execute your strategies and navigate challenges as you launch and grow your business.

Chapter 3: Building a Scalable Model

Creating a scalable business model is crucial for long-term growth and success. A scalable model allows your business to handle increased demand without a proportional increase in costs, ensuring that growth is sustainable and profitable. Here's how to build a scalable model:

1.   Design efficient processes.

Standardisation: Develop standard operating procedures (SOPs) for all critical processes. Standardisation ensures consistency, quality, and efficiency as the business grows.

Automation: Leverage technology to automate repetitive and time-consuming tasks. Automation reduces errors, saves time, and allows your team to focus on more strategic activities.

2.   Leverage Technology

Software Solutions: Invest in scalable software solutions for customer relationship management (CRM), enterprise resource planning (ERP), and project management. These tools streamline operations and provide valuable data insights.

Cloud Computing: Use cloud-based services to scale your IT infrastructure as needed. Cloud solutions offer flexibility, reduce costs, and provide access to advanced technologies.

3.   Build a strong team.

Hiring Strategy: Focus on hiring skilled and adaptable employees who can grow with the company. Prioritise roles that are critical to scaling operations.

Training and Development: Invest in continuous training and professional development to enhance your team's capabilities and keep them aligned with your business goals.

4.   Outsource non-core activities.

Strategic Outsourcing: Identify non-core activities that can be outsourced to third-party providers. This approach allows you to focus on your core competencies while benefiting from the expertise and efficiency of specialised service providers.

5. Expand Market Reach

Geographic Expansion: Explore new markets and regions to increase your customer base. Conduct thorough market research to identify potential opportunities and tailor your offerings to local needs.

Digital Marketing: Utilise digital marketing strategies to reach a broader audience. Social media, search engine optimization (SEO), and content marketing can significantly increase your brand's visibility and attract new customers.

6. Develop scalable revenue streams.

Recurring Revenue: Create subscription-based or recurring revenue models that provide predictable and stable income. Examples include SaaS products, membership programs, and service contracts.

Diversification: Diversify your product or service offerings to cater to different customer segments and reduce dependency on a single revenue stream.

7. Monitor and adjust

Data-Driven Decisions: Use data analytics to monitor performance, identify trends, and make informed decisions. Regularly review key performance indicators (KPIs) to assess scalability and make necessary adjustments.

Feedback Loops: Establish feedback loops with customers and employees to gather insights and continuously improve processes, products, and services.

By focusing on these key areas, you can build a scalable model that supports sustainable growth, enhances operational efficiency, and maximises profitability. Scalability ensures that your business can adapt to changing market conditions, meet increasing demand, and achieve long-term success without being constrained by resource limitations.

Designing Scalable Processes

Designing scalable processes is essential for ensuring that your business can grow efficiently and sustainably. Scalable processes allow your operations to handle increased demand without a proportional rise in costs or complexity. Here are key steps to designing scalable processes:

1. Map Current Processes

Process Mapping: Document existing workflows and processes. Use flowcharts or diagrams to visualise each step and identify areas for improvement.

Identify Bottlenecks: Analyse the current processes to identify bottlenecks, inefficiencies, and repetitive tasks that hinder scalability.

2. Standardise Procedures

Create SOPs: Develop standard operating procedures (SOPs) for all key processes. SOPs ensure consistency, quality, and efficiency across the organisation.

Best Practices: Incorporate industry best practices into your SOPs to ensure optimal performance and compliance with standards.

3. Leverage Automation

Automate Repetitive Tasks: Use technology to automate repetitive and manual tasks. Automation tools such as robotic process automation (RPA) can streamline operations and reduce human error.

Integrate Systems: Ensure that your business systems (e.g., CRM, ERP, accounting software) are integrated. Seamless integration reduces data silos and enhances information flow across the organisation.

4. Optimise resource allocation.

Scalable Infrastructure: Invest in scalable infrastructure such as cloud computing, which allows you to adjust resources based on demand.

Flexible Workforce: Implement a flexible staffing model, such as part-time or contract workers, to manage fluctuating workloads without overburdening your permanent staff.

5.   Implement continuous improvement.

Feedback Mechanisms: Establish regular feedback loops with employees and customers to identify areas for process improvement.

Kaizen Approach: Adopt continuous improvement methodologies such as Kaizen to foster a culture of ongoing process enhancement.

6.   Use data analytics.

Performance Metrics: Define key performance indicators (KPIs) to measure process efficiency and effectiveness. Regularly monitor these metrics to track progress.

Predictive Analytics: Utilise predictive analytics to forecast future trends and demands, enabling proactive adjustments to processes.

7.   Plan for Scalability

Modular Design: Design processes in a modular fashion so they can be easily scaled up or down based on business needs.

Capacity Planning: Conduct capacity planning to ensure that your processes can handle increased volume without compromising performance or quality.

8.   Train and empower employees.

Comprehensive Training: Provide thorough training for employees on new processes and technologies. Well-trained employees are crucial for maintaining efficiency and quality as the business scales.

Empower Decision-Making: Empower employees to make decisions and suggest improvements, fostering a culture of ownership and accountability.

9.   Regularly review and update

Process Audits: Conduct regular audits of your processes to ensure they remain efficient and scalable.

Adapt to Change: Stay agile and be prepared to update processes in response to market changes, technological advancements, and business growth.

By implementing these steps, you can design processes that are not only efficient and effective but also capable of scaling with your business. Scalable processes enable your business to grow sustainably, maintain high levels of performance, and respond swiftly to changing market demands, ensuring long-term success and competitiveness.

Automation and systematisation

Automation and systematisation are vital for creating a scalable business, as they streamline operations, reduce errors, and free up time for strategic activities. Begin by identifying repetitive tasks such as data entry, customer follow-ups, and report generation that consume significant time and resources. Implement automation tools like CRM systems, project management software, and marketing platforms to handle these tasks efficiently. Ensure these tools integrate seamlessly to maintain data consistency across functions. Standardise procedures through detailed documentation of workflows and best practices, creating a robust framework that supports consistent performance. Regularly review and update automated systems to adapt to evolving business needs, ensuring sustained efficiency and scalability. This approach not only enhances productivity but also positions the business for sustained growth by enabling the team to focus on high-value, strategic initiatives.

Chapter 4: Developing Your Brand

Developing a strong brand is crucial for differentiating your business in a competitive market and creating lasting connections with your target audience. Here are key steps to developing your brand:

Define your brand identity.

Mission and Vision: Clearly articulate your business's mission and vision. These statements should reflect your core values and long-term goals.

Unique Value Proposition: Identify what sets your business apart from competitors. This unique value proposition should highlight the benefits and value your products or services offer.

Understand your target audience.

Market Research: Conduct thorough research to understand the demographics, preferences, and needs of your target audience.

Customer Personas: Develop detailed customer personas to represent your ideal customers. These personas help tailor your branding and marketing strategies to meet specific customer needs.

Create a visual identity.

Logo Design: Invest in a professional logo that reflects your brand's identity. It should be memorable, versatile, and consistent with your brand's values.

Color Scheme and Typography: Choose a colour palette and typography that align with your brand's personality. Consistent use of colours and fonts across all marketing materials enhances brand recognition.

Develop your brand voice.

Tone and Style: Define the tone and style of your brand's communication. Whether it's formal, friendly, authoritative, or playful, ensure it resonates with your target audience and remains consistent across all channels.

Messaging: Create key messaging points that convey your brand's values, mission, and unique value proposition. These messages should be used in marketing materials, social media, and customer interactions.

Build an online presence.

Website: Develop a professional, user-friendly website that serves as the hub of your online presence. It should clearly convey your brand's identity, offerings, and values.

Social Media: Leverage social media platforms to engage with your audience, share valuable content, and reinforce your brand's personality. Consistent branding across social media profiles is essential.

Deliver a consistent brand experience.

Customer Service: Ensure that every customer interaction reflects your brand's values and promises. Exceptional customer service enhances brand loyalty and reputation.

Packaging and Presentation: Pay attention to the packaging and presentation of your products. High-quality, branded packaging can leave a lasting impression on customers.

Monitor and evolve your brand.

Feedback and Analytics: Regularly gather feedback from customers and use analytics to monitor brand performance. This data helps identify areas for improvement and opportunities for growth.

Adapt and Innovate: Be willing to adapt and innovate your brand strategy as market conditions and customer preferences evolve. Staying relevant is key to long-term brand success.

By following these steps, you can develop a strong, cohesive brand that resonates with your target audience, differentiates your business, and fosters customer loyalty. A well-defined brand not only attracts new customers but also builds a community of advocates who support and promote your business.

Brand identity and positioning: Brand identity and positioning are fundamental elements of a successful business strategy.

Brand Identity

Brand identity encompasses the visual and experiential elements that define your brand in the minds of consumers. It includes your logo, colour scheme, typography, and overall design language, as well as the tone of voice and messaging used in communications. A strong brand identity is consistent across all touchpoints, creating a cohesive and recognizable presence. It should reflect your brand's core values, mission, and unique value proposition, making it stand out in a crowded market. A compelling brand identity not only attracts customers but also builds trust and loyalty, as it conveys professionalism and reliability.

Brand Positioning

Brand positioning, on the other hand, refers to how your brand is perceived in the minds of your target audience relative to competitors. It involves defining the key benefits and differentiators that make your brand unique. Effective positioning requires a deep understanding of your target market's needs, preferences, and pain points. Your positioning statement should clearly articulate the unique value your brand offers and why it is the best choice for your customers. This involves highlighting specific attributes, benefits, or experiences that set your brand apart.

By integrating a strong brand identity with strategic positioning, you can create a powerful brand presence that resonates with your audience, fosters loyalty, and drives business growth. These elements ensure your brand communicates a clear, consistent, and compelling message that stands out in the competitive landscape.

Crafting Your Brand Story

A compelling brand story is a powerful tool that can differentiate your business, connect with your audience emotionally, and build lasting loyalty. Here's how to craft an effective brand story:

Understand your core values and mission.

Your brand story should reflect your business's core values and mission. Clearly define what your business stands for and why it exists. This foundation will help you create a story that resonates authentically with your audience.

Identify your brand's origin.

Every great story has a beginning. Describe how your business started, the challenges you faced, and the inspiration behind your venture. Sharing your origin story humanises your brand and makes it relatable to your audience.

Highlight key milestones.

Identify significant events and achievements in your business journey. These milestones could include product launches, major partnerships, awards, or pivotal moments that shaped your business. Highlighting these points adds depth and credibility to your story.

Showcase your unique value proposition.

Explain what makes your brand unique and why customers should choose you over competitors. Your brand story should emphasise the unique value your products or services offer and how they solve specific problems or meet customer needs.

Incorporate customer success stories.

Include testimonials or stories from satisfied customers who have benefited from your products or services. Real-life examples of how your business has positively impacted others make your brand story more compelling and trustworthy.

Use authentic and engaging language.

Your brand story should be told in a voice that reflects your brand's personality. Whether it's casual, professional, humorous, or serious, ensure that the tone aligns with your overall branding. Use engaging language that captivates your audience and keeps them interested.

Create emotional connections.

Emotional connections drive customer loyalty. Share experiences, challenges, and victories that evoke emotions. Whether it's overcoming adversity, achieving a significant breakthrough, or making a positive impact, these elements can resonate deeply with your audience.

Keep it consistent across channels.

Ensure that your brand story is consistent across all communication channels, including your website, social media, marketing materials, and customer interactions. Consistency helps reinforce your brand message and build a cohesive identity.

Be honest and transparent.

Authenticity is crucial to building trust. Be honest and transparent about your journey, including the ups and downs. Customers appreciate brands that are genuine and open about their experiences.

End your brand story with a call to action. Encourage your audience to engage with your brand, whether it's by visiting your website, following you on social media, or trying your products or services.

By crafting a compelling brand story that incorporates these elements, you can create a narrative that not only differentiates your brand but also fosters strong emotional connections with your audience. A well-told brand story can drive customer loyalty, enhance your brand's reputation, and ultimately contribute to the long-term success of your business.

Chapter 5: Building a Strong Team

Building a strong team is fundamental to the success of any business. A cohesive, motivated, and skilled team can drive innovation, productivity, and growth. Here are the essential steps to building a strong team:

1. Define clear roles and responsibilities.

Job Descriptions: Create detailed job descriptions that outline the specific roles, responsibilities, and expectations for each position.

Role Clarity: Ensure that each team member understands their role and how it contributes to the overall goals of the organisation.

2. Hire the right people.

Cultural Fit: Hire individuals who align with your company's values and culture. A good cultural fit enhances teamwork and morale.

Skills and Experience: Prioritise candidates with the necessary skills and experience, but also consider the potential for growth and development.

Diverse Talent: Aim for diversity in skills, backgrounds, and perspectives to foster innovation and problem-solving.

3. Foster a positive work environment.

Open Communication: Encourage open and honest communication. Create channels for team members to share ideas, feedback, and concerns.

Collaboration: Promote a collaborative culture where teamwork and collective problem-solving are valued.

Respect and Inclusion: Ensure a respectful and inclusive environment where all team members feel valued and heard.

4. Provide training and development.

Onboarding: Implement a comprehensive onboarding process to integrate new hires effectively.

Continuous Learning: Offer ongoing training and development opportunities to help employees enhance their skills and advance their careers.

Mentorship: Establish mentorship programs where experienced employees can guide and support newer team members.

5. Set clear goals and expectations.

Smart Goals: Set specific, measurable, achievable, relevant, and time-bound (SMART) goals for the team and individual members.

Regular Feedback: Provide regular feedback on performance, acknowledging achievements, and addressing areas for improvement.

6. Recognize and reward achievement.

Incentives and Rewards: Implement a system to recognize and reward outstanding performance. This can include bonuses, promotions, and other incentives.

Public Acknowledgment: Celebrate successes publicly within the organisation to boost morale and motivation.

7. Encourage work-life balance.

Flexible Schedules: Offer flexible working hours or remote work options to help employees balance their professional and personal lives.

Wellness Programs: Promote health and wellness through initiatives such as gym memberships, mental health support, and wellness workshops.

8. Build trust and accountability.

Trust Building: Foster trust through transparency, consistency, and reliability in leadership and team interactions.

Accountability: Hold team members accountable for their responsibilities and performance, ensuring that everyone contributes to the team's success.

9. Promote team-building activities.

Team Events: Organise team-building activities, such as retreats, workshops, and social events, to strengthen relationships and teamwork.

Problem-Solving Exercises: Engage in collaborative exercises that encourage team members to work together to solve challenges.

10. Evaluate and adapt.
Regular Assessments: Conduct regular assessments of team performance and dynamics.

Adaptability: Be willing to adapt strategies and approaches based on feedback and the changing needs of the team.

By focusing on these key areas, you can build a strong, cohesive team that drives your business forward. A well-constructed team not only enhances productivity and innovation but also creates a positive work environment where employees are motivated to achieve their best.

Hiring the right people

Hiring the right people is crucial for the success and growth of any business. The right hires not only possess the necessary skills and experience but also fit well with the company culture and values, contributing positively to the team dynamic. Here are some key considerations and strategies for hiring the right people:

Define the role clearly.

Start with a detailed job description that outlines the responsibilities, required skills, and qualifications for the role. Clearly defined roles help attract candidates who are well-suited for the job and reduce misunderstandings about job expectations.

Cultural Fit

Assessing cultural fit is as important as evaluating technical skills. Employees who align with your company's values and culture are more likely to contribute positively to the work environment and stay with the company for longer. During interviews, ask questions that reveal the candidate's values, work style, and how they handle various situations.

Use multiple recruitment channels.
Diversify your recruitment efforts by using various channels, such as job boards, social media, employee referrals, and recruitment agencies. Each channel can reach different types of candidates, increasing your chances of finding the right fit.

Structured Interviews

Conduct structured interviews to ensure a fair and consistent evaluation process. Prepare a set of standard questions for all candidates, focusing on both technical competencies and behavioural traits. This approach helps in comparing candidates objectively.

Skills Assessment

Incorporate practical assessments or tasks relevant to the job during the recruitment process. Skills assessments provide a clear picture of the candidate's abilities and how they apply their skills in real-world scenarios.

Reference Checks

Always perform thorough reference checks to verify the candidate's past performance and work ethic. Speaking with former employers or colleagues can provide valuable insights that are not always evident during the interview process.

Emphasise growth potential.

While experience is important, also consider the candidate's potential for growth within the company. Hiring individuals who are eager to learn and develop can be beneficial in the long term, as they can adapt and take on more responsibilities as the business evolves.

Candidate Experience

Ensure a positive candidate experience throughout the recruitment process. Communicate clearly, provide timely updates, and be respectful of their time. A positive experience reflects well on your company and can attract top talent.

Diversity and inclusion

Prioritise diversity and inclusion in your hiring practices. A diverse workforce brings varied perspectives and ideas, fostering innovation and creativity. Implement unbiased hiring practices to ensure you are selecting the best candidates based on merit.

Onboarding and Integration

Once you've hired the right people, invest in a robust onboarding process to help new employees integrate smoothly into the team. Effective onboarding ensures that new hires feel welcomed, understand their roles, and are set up for success from the start.

By focusing on these strategies, you can build a team of skilled, motivated, and culturally aligned employees who will drive your business forward. The right hires not only enhance productivity and innovation but also contribute to a positive and dynamic work environment.

Defining roles and responsibilities

Defining roles and responsibilities is a critical step in building a successful and efficient team. Clear roles and responsibilities ensure that everyone knows what is expected of them, reduce overlap and confusion, and increase accountability and productivity. Here's how to effectively define roles and responsibilities:

1. Understand business goals and needs.

Identify Key Objectives: Start by understanding your business goals and what needs to be accomplished. This will help you determine the key roles necessary to achieve these objectives.

Assess Current Resources: Evaluate your current team's skills and workload to identify gaps and areas where new roles might be needed.

2. Create detailed job descriptions.

Title and Summary: Begin with a clear job title and a brief summary of the role.

Duties and Responsibilities: List the specific tasks and responsibilities associated with the role. Be as detailed as possible to provide a clear picture of what the job entails.

Required Skills and Qualifications: Outline the essential skills, qualifications, and experience needed for the role. Include any certifications or specialised knowledge required.

Reporting Structure: Specify who the role reports to and any supervisory responsibilities.

3. Define key performance indicators (KPIs).

Set Measurable Goals: Establish clear, measurable goals and KPIs for each role. These should align with the overall business objectives and provide a way to assess performance.

Regular Reviews: Schedule regular performance reviews to discuss progress, provide feedback, and adjust responsibilities as needed.

4. Ensure role clarity.

Avoid Overlaps: Clearly delineate responsibilities to avoid overlap and ensure that each team member knows their specific duties.

Communicate Expectations: Hold meetings to communicate roles and responsibilities to the entire team. Ensure everyone understands their role and how it fits into the larger organisational structure.

5. Document and Share

Role Manuals: Create role manuals or guides that detail responsibilities, processes, and best practices for each position.

Accessible Information: Ensure that these documents are easily accessible to all team members, either through a shared drive, intranet, or company handbook.

6. Foster collaboration and flexibility.

Encourage teamwork: While roles should be clearly defined, encourage collaboration and support among team members. Flexibility can be beneficial, especially in dynamic or project-based environments.

Adaptability: Be open to evolving roles and responsibilities as the business grows and changes. Regularly reassess roles to ensure they remain aligned with business needs.

7. Provide training and support.

Ongoing Training: Offer training and development opportunities to help employees excel in their roles and adapt to new responsibilities.

Support Systems: Establish support systems, such as mentoring programs, to help new hires and existing employees navigate their roles effectively.

8. Feedback and Improvement

Regular Check-ins: Conduct regular check-ins with team members to discuss their roles, address any challenges, and make necessary adjustments.

Solicit Feedback: Encourage employees to provide feedback on their roles and responsibilities. Use this feedback to make improvements and enhance role clarity.

By following these steps, you can ensure that roles and responsibilities are clearly defined, understood, and aligned with your business objectives. Clear roles and responsibilities not only enhance individual performance but also improve overall team cohesion and efficiency, contributing to the success and growth of your business.

Chapter 6: Customer Acquisition and Retention

Effective customer acquisition and retention strategies are essential for sustainable business growth. While acquiring new customers expands your market reach, retaining existing ones ensures long-term profitability and loyalty.

Customer Acquisition

Customer acquisition involves attracting new customers to your business.

Identify your target audience.

Market Research: Conduct thorough market research to understand the demographics, preferences, and pain points of your potential customers.

Customer Personas: Develop detailed customer personas to represent different segments of your target audience. These personas help tailor your marketing strategies to meet specific needs.

Develop a strong value proposition.

Unique Value: Clearly articulate what makes your product or service unique and why it's the best choice for customers. Your value proposition should address how your offering solves a problem or fulfils a need.

Utilise multiple marketing channels.

Digital Marketing: Leverage SEO, content marketing, social media, email marketing, and online advertising to reach a broader audience.

Offline Marketing: Use traditional methods like print ads, direct mail, events, and trade shows to capture attention.

Partnerships and referrals: Collaborate with other businesses and encourage satisfied customers to refer others, leveraging the power of word-of-mouth marketing.

Optimise your sales funnel.

Lead Generation: Use tactics like lead magnets, webinars, and free trials to attract potential customers.

Nurturing Leads: Implement email marketing and CRM systems to nurture leads through personalised communication and targeted content.

Conversion: Ensure a seamless and user-friendly purchase process to convert leads into customers.

Analyse and adjust

Analytics Tools: Use tools like Google Analytics, CRM systems, and social media analytics to monitor the performance of your acquisition strategies.

Continuous Improvement: Regularly review data and adjust your tactics based on insights to improve effectiveness and ROI.

Customer Retention

Customer retention focuses on keeping existing customers engaged and satisfied, encouraging repeat business, and fostering loyalty. Here's how to improve retention:

Deliver exceptional customer service.

Responsive Support: Provide prompt and effective customer support through various channels such as phone, email, live chat, and social media.

Customer Satisfaction: Train your team to handle inquiries and resolve issues efficiently, ensuring a positive customer experience.

Personalise the customer experience.

Customer Data: Use customer data to personalise interactions and recommendations. Tailored communication can enhance customer satisfaction and loyalty.

Psychographic Data: Explore the lifestyle, values, interests, and attitudes of your audience. Psychographic data provides insights into what motivates your customers and how they make decisions.

Behavioural Data: Analyse customer behaviours, including purchasing patterns, brand loyalty, and product usage. Behavioural data helps identify the actions your customers take and how they interact with your brand.

Create detailed customer personas.

Persona Development: Develop detailed customer personas that represent different segments of your target audience. Each persona should include demographic, geographic, psychographic, and behavioural characteristics.

Persona Profiles: Create profiles for each persona, including a name, background, goals, challenges, and preferences. These profiles help personalise your marketing strategies and communications.

Analyse your current customer base.

Customer Data: Review your existing customer data to identify common characteristics and trends. Look at purchase history, feedback, and engagement metrics.

Segmentation: Segment your current customers into different groups based on their characteristics and behaviours. This helps identify the most valuable segments to target.

Conduct surveys and interviews.

Surveys: Use online surveys to gather information from your audience. Ask questions about their preferences, needs, challenges, and demographics.

Interviews: Conduct in-depth interviews with existing customers and potential customers. Interviews provide qualitative insights that can uncover deeper motivations and pain points.

Analyse competitor audiences.

Competitor Research: Study your competitors to understand who their customers are. Analyse their marketing strategies, customer reviews, and social media engagement.

Benchmarking: Compare your findings with those of your own target audience to identify overlaps and gaps. This can help you refine your audience targeting.

Leverage analytics tools

Web Analytics: Use tools like Google Analytics to analyse website traffic and user behaviour. This data can reveal valuable information about your audience's demographics, interests, and online habits.

Social Media Analytics: Utilise social media analytics to understand the demographics and behaviours of your followers and engaged users. Social media platforms provide insights into audience interests and engagement levels.

Refine and segment your audience.

Segmentation Criteria: Refine your target audience by segmenting them based on specific criteria such as age, location, buying behaviour, or interest. This allows you to create more targeted and effective marketing campaigns.

Prioritise Segments: Identify the most valuable segments based on factors such as market size, profitability, and alignment with your business goals.

Test and iterate.

A/B Testing: Conduct A/B testing on different marketing messages and strategies to see which resonates best with your target audience.

Feedback Loop: Continuously gather feedback from your audience and analyse the results. Use this feedback to refine your understanding of your target audience and adjust your strategies accordingly.

By following these steps, you can gain a comprehensive understanding of your target audience. Knowing who your customers are, what they need, and how they behave enables you to create more personalised and effective marketing strategies. This not only improves customer acquisition and retention but also enhances overall customer satisfaction and business performance.

Chapter 7: Financial Management

Financial management is a cornerstone of business success, encompassing the strategic planning, organising, directing, and controlling of financial activities. Effective financial management ensures that an organisation efficiently uses its resources to achieve its goals, maintain solvency, and maximise profitability. Here are the key components and best practices of financial management:

1. Budgeting and planning

Budget Creation: Develop detailed budgets that outline expected revenues and expenses. Budgets help in setting financial targets and guiding spending decisions.

Financial Forecasting: Use historical data and market trends to predict future financial performance. Forecasting helps in anticipating challenges and opportunities, enabling proactive management.

2. Cash Flow Management

Monitor Cash Flow: Regularly track the inflow and outflow of cash to ensure that the business has sufficient liquidity to meet its obligations. Cash flow statements provide insights into operating, investing, and financing activities.

Optimise Working Capital: Manage inventory, receivables, and payables efficiently to maintain a healthy cash flow. Strategies include negotiating favourable credit terms and timely collection of receivables.

3. Financial Analysis and Reporting

Financial Statements: Prepare and analyse key financial statements, including the income statement, balance sheet, and cash flow statement. These documents provide a comprehensive view of the business's financial health.

Ratio Analysis: Use financial ratios to assess profitability, liquidity, solvency, and efficiency. Common ratios include the current ratio, debt-to-equity ratio, and return on equity.

4. Investment Decisions

Capital Budgeting: Evaluate potential investment opportunities using techniques such as net present value (NPV), internal rate of return (IRR), and payback period. This ensures that investments align with the company's strategic goals and provide adequate returns.

Risk Management: Assess and manage financial risks associated with investments. Diversification and hedging strategies can mitigate risks.

5. Cost control and efficiency

Cost Analysis: Regularly review costs to identify areas where expenses can be reduced without compromising quality. Implement cost-saving measures such as process improvements and bulk purchasing.

Benchmarking: Compare financial performance against industry standards and competitors to identify areas for improvement.

6. Funding and Capital Structure

Funding Sources: Explore various funding options, including equity, debt, and internal financing. Choose the appropriate mix based on cost of capital, risk tolerance, and financial flexibility.

Capital Structure Management: Maintain an optimal balance between debt and equity to minimise the cost of capital while ensuring financial stability.

7. Regulatory Compliance

Adhere to Regulations: Ensure compliance with financial regulations and standards such as GAAP or IFRS. Regular audits and transparent financial reporting build trust with stakeholders.

Tax Management: Optimise tax liabilities through effective tax planning and compliance. Understand and leverage available tax credits and deductions.

8. Technology and automation

Financial Software: Use financial management software to automate processes, improve accuracy, and gain real-time insights into financial performance.

Data Analytics: Leverage data analytics to make informed financial decisions. Advanced analytics can uncover trends, forecast outcomes, and enhance strategic planning.

Effective financial management is integral to sustaining business growth, enhancing operational efficiency, and ensuring long-term profitability. By implementing these practices, businesses can make informed decisions, manage risks, and achieve their financial objectives.

Accounting and bookkeeping

Accounting and bookkeeping are essential functions in any business, ensuring accurate financial records and compliance with financial regulations. Bookkeeping involves the systematic recording of financial transactions, including sales, purchases, income, and payments. This process forms the foundation of the accounting system. Key bookkeeping tasks include maintaining ledgers, journals, and receipts, which provide detailed documentation of every transaction.

Accounting, on the other hand, involves interpreting, classifying, analysing, reporting, and summarising financial data. Accountants prepare financial statements such as the balance sheet, income statement, and cash flow statement, which offer insights into the financial health of the business. They also handle tax filings, audit preparation, and strategic financial planning.

Together, accounting and bookkeeping ensure that businesses have a clear and accurate picture of their financial situation, enabling informed decision-making, efficient financial management, and compliance with legal requirements. These practices are vital for tracking financial performance, managing budgets, and supporting long-term growth strategies.

Setting up financial systems

Setting up financial systems is a crucial step for any business to ensure accurate, efficient, and transparent financial management. A well-designed financial system streamlines processes, enhances decision-making, and ensures regulatory compliance. Here are the key components and steps involved:

1. Choosing the Right Software

Accounting Software: Select robust accounting software tailored to your business needs. Popular options include QuickBooks, Xero, and FreshBooks, which offer functionalities such as invoicing, expense tracking, payroll management, and financial reporting.

Integration Capabilities: Ensure the software integrates with other business systems like CRM, inventory management, and banking platforms for seamless data flow and reduced manual entry.

2. Chart of Accounts

Define Accounts: Create a comprehensive chart of accounts that categorises all financial transactions. This should include accounts for assets, liabilities, equity, revenues, and expenses, providing a clear structure for financial reporting.

Customization: Tailor the chart of accounts to match the specific needs and nature of your business, ensuring it reflects your financial activities accurately.

3. Internal Controls

Segregation of Duties: Implement internal controls to prevent fraud and errors. Segregate duties so that no single individual handles all aspects of a financial transaction.

Approval Processes: Establish approval processes for financial transactions such as expenditures, payroll, and vendor payments to ensure oversight and accountability.

4. Document Management

Record-keeping: Set up a system for organising and storing financial documents, including invoices, receipts, bank statements, and tax records. Digital solutions can enhance accessibility and security.

Compliance: Ensure that your document management system complies with legal requirements for record retention and data privacy.

5. Financial Reporting

Standard Reports: Generate regular financial reports, including income statements, balance sheets, and cash flow statements. These reports provide insights into your business's financial health and performance.

Customised Reports: Develop customised reports to meet specific business needs, such as budget variance reports or departmental profit and loss statements.

6. Training and support

Employee Training: Train staff on the financial systems and procedures to ensure accurate data entry and adherence to protocols.

Ongoing Support: Provide ongoing support and resources to address any issues or updates needed in the financial system.

By setting up effective financial systems, businesses can enhance accuracy, improve financial control, and facilitate strategic planning. This foundation supports sustainable growth and ensures that financial information is readily available for decision-making and compliance purposes.

Chapter 8: Sustaining Growth and Adapting

Sustaining growth and adapting to changing market conditions are essential for long-term business success. To sustain growth, businesses must continuously innovate, improve efficiency, and expand their market reach. This involves investing in research and development, embracing new technologies, and refining business processes. Additionally, focusing on customer satisfaction and retention through excellent service and value propositions can lead to repeat business and referrals.

Adapting to change requires agility and a proactive approach. Businesses should regularly analyse market trends, customer needs, and competitive landscapes to anticipate shifts and respond effectively. This might involve diversifying product lines, entering new markets, or revising business models. Building a flexible organisational structure and fostering a culture of continuous improvement and learning can help businesses stay resilient and capitalise on new opportunities. Through sustained innovation, strategic planning, and adaptability, businesses can maintain growth and thrive in a dynamic environment.

Strategies for long-term growth

Long-term growth requires a strategic approach that encompasses innovation, market expansion, customer focus, and operational excellence. Here are key strategies to achieve sustained growth:

Innovation and Product Development

Continuous Improvement: Regularly update and improve products and services based on customer feedback and market research.

Research and Development: Invest in R&D to create new offerings that meet emerging needs and leverage technological advancements.

Market Expansion

Geographic Expansion: Enter new markets, both domestically and internationally, to increase your customer base and revenue streams.

Diversification: Introduce new product lines or services that complement your existing offerings to attract a broader audience.

Customer Focus

Customer Experience: Enhance the customer experience by providing exceptional service, personalised interactions, and value-added features.

Loyalty Programs: Implement loyalty programs to reward repeat customers and foster long-term relationships.

4. Operational Efficiency

Process Optimization: Streamline operations through process improvements, automation, and adopting best practices.

Cost Management: Regularly review and manage costs to maintain profitability while scaling operations.

Strategic Partnerships

Alliances and Collaborations: Form strategic partnerships and alliances to leverage complementary strengths, share resources, and enter new markets.

Joint Ventures: Engage in joint ventures to pool expertise and resources for mutual growth.

Digital Transformation

Adopt Technology: Embrace digital tools and platforms to enhance efficiency, improve customer engagement, and drive innovation.

Data-Driven Decisions: Utilise data analytics to inform strategic decisions, identify growth opportunities, and measure performance.

Employee Development

Training and Development: Invest in employee training and development to build a skilled, motivated workforce.

Culture of Innovation: Foster a culture that encourages creativity, innovation, and continuous learning.

Financial Planning

Capital Management: Secure adequate funding to support growth initiatives, whether through reinvestment of profits, external financing, or strategic investments.

Risk Management: Identify and mitigate potential risks through proactive risk management strategies.

By implementing these strategies, businesses can build a solid foundation for long-term growth, ensuring they remain competitive, resilient, and capable of adapting to changing market dynamics.

Expanding your market reach

Expanding your market reach is vital for business growth and sustainability. It involves broadening your customer base and increasing your presence in existing or new markets. Here are several strategies to achieve this:

Market Penetration

Enhancing Visibility: Increase brand awareness through targeted marketing campaigns, social media engagement, and search engine optimization (SEO).

Competitive Pricing: Offer competitive pricing or promotional discounts to attract new customers and increase market share.

Geographic Expansion

Entering New Regions: Explore and enter new geographic markets, both domestically and internationally. Conduct thorough market research to understand local preferences and regulations.

Local Partnerships: Form partnerships with local businesses to gain insights and access to new markets.

Product Diversification

New Products and Services: Develop and introduce new products or services that cater to different customer needs or market segments.

Customization: Offer customised solutions to meet specific regional or demographic demands.

Digital Transformation

E-commerce Platforms: Leverage e-commerce platforms to reach a global audience. Ensure your online presence is robust and user-friendly.

Online Advertising: Utilise online advertising tools such as Google Ads and social media ads to target specific audiences and drive traffic to your website.

Customer Referrals

Referral Programs: Implement referral programs that incentivize existing customers to refer new ones. Word-of-mouth can be a powerful tool for expanding your reach.

By implementing these strategies, businesses can effectively expand their market reach, attract new customers, and achieve sustainable growth in a competitive environment.

Conclusion:

Building a business, not a job, requires a mindset shift from being an employee to being an entrepreneur. It demands taking calculated risks, innovating, and creating value. By focusing on building a sustainable business, you can achieve financial freedom, scalability, and a lasting legacy.

Remember, building a business is a marathon, not a sprint. Stay committed, resilient, and focused on your vision.